IMAGES
of America

DUBLIN
THE EMERALD CITY

GREETINGS FROM DUBLIN, GA. During the heyday of postcard collecting in the early 20th century, greeting cards in the poppy pattern were popular with collectors. Shown in the photograph clockwise from the top are the city hall, the courthouse, the library, Bellevue Avenue, and a freight boat on the Oconee River.

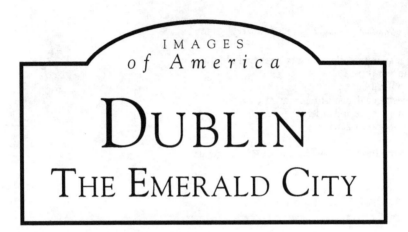

IMAGES
of America

DUBLIN
THE EMERALD CITY

Scott Thompson

ARCADIA
PUBLISHING

Published by Arcadia Publishing
Charleston SC, Chicago IL, Portsmouth NH, San Francisco CA

Library of Congress Catalog Card Number: 00-104297

For all general information contact Arcadia Publishing at:
Telephone 843-853-2070
Fax 843-853-0044
E-Mail sales@arcadiapublishing.com
For customer service and orders:
Toll-Free 1-888-313-2665

Visit us on the Internet at www.arcadiapublishing.com

First National Bank Building,
Dublin Ga.

THE FIRST NATIONAL BANK. Known as "Dublin's skyscraper," the First National Bank, which was completed in May 1913, was the crown jewel of the "Emerald City."

4

CONTENTS

Acknowledgments   6

Introduction   7

1.   The Emerald City   9

2.   Bellevue Avenue   49

3.   Transportation   59

4.   Our Churches   69

5.   Our Schools   77

6.   Life in the Emerald City   85

7.   Leaders of the Emerald City   119

ACKNOWLEDGMENTS

Two decades ago I began collecting postcards. I was fascinated by the scenes of Dublin they depicted—they were familiar, yet so vastly different, from our current lifestyles. Some of the houses and buildings in the pictures were long gone but some remained, and I was hooked. My collection has grown to nearly 7,000 cards from the state of Georgia alone. They say "A picture is worth a thousand words," but in many cases, they are worth so much more. Many of the photographs in this book are one of a kind. Very few were kept at home, and in some cases there may be less than ten of a particular card known to exist.

Six years ago, I received a call from an elderly Macon man. He had seen a newspaper article about my interest in Dublin's history. Mack Jordan and his father, E.R. Jordan, had kept a stack of nearly 100 photographs of Dublin for over 80 years. He wanted them to have a home. Mr. Jordan brought them to me. Most of them were real photo postcards, which were taken by local photographer Doyle Knight and sold to tourists. As our conversation progressed, I soon discovered that Mr. Jordan grew up in the house next door to where I live. After he left Dublin in the 1920s, he moved to Macon. His best friend there was Billy Stubbs. Guess what? Billy Stubbs was my great uncle.

My love of the history of Dublin was cultivated through my relationship with the Main Street Program. As chairman of Main Street Dublin, the Downtown Development Authority, I began to take notice of the treasures we have in the downtown area and realized that many of these have been lost, along with the grand old houses—victims to the modern commercial buildings.

The city of Dublin underwent a phoenix-like transformation during its "Golden Era." In the mid-1880s, alcohol was strangling the residents of Dublin, and people were ashamed of their town. As the railroads eventually made their way into the area, the town began to grow, slowly at first and then meteorically for nearly two decades. Dublin went from a sleepy stagnant village to one of the premier cities in Georgia.

I gratefully acknowledge the accomplishments of the people of the Emerald City. Their contributions to the quality of life in our city have lasted for more than a century. I especially thank the photographers who supplied the images for this book. I thank the historians along with the directors, members, and friends of the Laurens County Historical Society, which is the repository for most of these precious photographs. A special thanks to Trudy Lord and Betty Page for their thoughtful and detailed organization and descriptions of the photographs.

Finally, for their friendship, advice, and encouragement, I thank John Ross, Hon. Allen Thomas, Rev. Joan Kilian, Dr. John C. Belcher, and Rep. Dubose Porter. For their patience and love, I thank my wife, Mary Beth, my son Scotty, and my parents, Jane and Dale Thompson.

INTRODUCTION

In the mid-1880s, there was trouble in the Emerald City. Dublin was burdened with crime, mainly as a result of the heavy consumption of alcohol in public barrooms. Civic and religious leaders came together and eventually eliminated the legal sale of alcohol. Dublin was still without a railroad until 1886, when the Wrightsville & Tennille Railroad was completed to the east side of the river. The shakeup in Dublin's stagnation as a town began with the coming of the railroad, which nearly coincided with the great Charleston earthquake of August 31, 1886. In the pre-dawn hours of May 26, 1889, a fire broke out in a storehouse near the post office. Five hours later, ten business houses and the post office had been destroyed.

The year 1891 was one of the most important in the history of the city. Four events signaled the beginning of the explosive growth of Dublin's Golden Era. The Wrightsville & Tennille Railroad completed a concrete railroad bridge over the river. The railroad's bridge was constructed near the first permanent passenger bridge, which had just been completed. The construction of the bridges was followed by the completion of the Macon, Dublin, & Savannah Railroad into Dublin. New communities sprang up along the main railroads. These railroad boom towns allowed more access to the markets in Dublin. A third railroad, the Empire & Dublin Railroad, later known as the Oconee & Western, came to Dublin in 1891. The fifth railroad to run through Dublin, the Dublin & Southwestern, was completed to Eastman in 1905.

Dublin, at the intersection of five railroads, exploded almost overnight. With the prohibition of liquor sales, Dublin had outgrown its image as a lawless and violent community. The railroads brought in new industries. Despite the coming of the railroads, river traffic continued to flourish. Downtown Dublin was filled with all types of mercantile stores from department stores to dry goods to grocery stores. The Georgia Warehouse and Compress Company was completed in 1895. The Dublin Telegraph and Telephone Exchange was established in 1897. The city of Dublin established its own power plant, bringing the first electric lights into homes and businesses.

During the first decade of the 20th century, Dublin was the third-fastest growing city in Georgia. It grew so fast that boosters described it as "The only town in Georgia, that's doublin all the time." People by the thousands, from several states and countries, came into a town that only numbered a few hundred two decades before. Religious and ethnic diversity was increasing.

Two banks were organized in Dublin in 1898. Before the period of economic growth ended, Dublin would be home to seven banks. The businessmen of Dublin organized the Young Men's Business League in 1900, which became the Dublin Chamber of Commerce in 1911. Dublin hosted more than a dozen state conventions during the period. The citizens of Dublin built the first library in 1904 with the aid of philanthropist Andrew Carnegie. The first automobile came in 1902, thrilling onlookers and frightening horses. Stubbs Park, designed by renowned horticulturist P.J. Berckmans, opened in 1909. The streets and sidewalks of Dublin saw vast improvements. At the end of the 20th century's first decade, electric street lights began to appear on the downtown streets.

The Chautauqua Festival was the main entertainment event every summer from 1902 to 1909. The community built a large wooden auditorium on the southwest corner of West Madison and South Monroe Streets to house the festival and other community events. The Bertha Theatre (1913–1918), the largest auditorium ever built in Dublin, was the site of many of the country's best traveling musical and vaudeville shows and the first talking pictures in 1913. The first 12th Congressional District Fair was held in the store building of the Gilbert Hardware Company in 1911. The fair, which attracted several thousands of visitors each year, eventually moved to its permanent site on Telfair Street. Judge W.W. Larsen was elected to Congress in 1916. The New York Yankees defeated the Boston Braves in a closely fought game at the 12th District Fairgrounds on Telfair Street in 1918. Rev. W.N. Ainsworth, who served First Methodist Church, was elected bishop of the Methodist Episcopal Church South.

Many African-American Dubliners and Laurens Countians began to prosper during this period. Property ownership increased along with total wealth. Rev. W.A. Dinkins founded the Dublin Normal Industrial College on East Jackson Street in 1905. In 1909, the CME Church of Georgia established the Harriet Holsey Industrial College in the Scottsville community. It was Dublin's first college. Three physicians, B.D. Perry, U.S. Johnson, and H.T. Jones, came to Dublin to set up their practices. Susie White Dasher led the improvement of education in African-American schools.

Dublin and Laurens County furnished nearly 1,100 men to the armed forces in World War I. Dubliners contributed to the war through bond sales. James Mason died in France on July 29, 1918—making him the first Dubliner to die in action. James L. Weddington Jr. was awarded the French Croix de Guerre on July 10, 1918, for his heroism in carrying many wounded men off the battle field to field hospitals for several hours, risking his own safety in the process. Fortunately, the war was relatively short and only 50 Laurens County men lost their lives. After the war, the Dublin Guards were reorganized into the Georgia National Guard, the first unit in the southeastern United States.

The months after the war were devastating. Dublin and Laurens County depended on the cotton crop. Laurens, a perennial leader in the production of cotton, led the state in production from 1911 through 1913. In 1911, the county produced well over 61,000 bales (over 30 million pounds of cotton), which brought in untold amounts of income to Dublin merchants.

The coming of the boll weevil, the influenza epidemic of 1918, and World War I brought about an end to the first Golden Age of the Emerald City. Now, at the beginning of the 21st century, Dublin is well into its second Golden Age.

One

THE EMERALD CITY

WEST JACKSON STREET. This photograph, c. 1920, shows the main street of Dublin in a view taken from the courthouse tower. On the left is the Stubbs Leitch Building and on the right is the R.C. Henry Building. The old brick water tower dominates the western skyline of the city.

THE LAURENS COUNTY COURTHOUSE, 1895–1962. This courthouse, built in 1895, was designed by the firm of Morgan & Dillon. The courthouse was also used for community events, church services, and political gatherings. Nearly every leading Georgia politician made an appearance at the courthouse during the Golden Era. It was razed in 1963 and replaced by a modern courthouse, which was the first federally funded county courthouse in the U.S.

THE LAURENS COUNTY COURTHOUSE, 1845–1895. This two-story wooden building was the third courthouse on the courthouse square. During the days of Reconstruction following the Civil War, the courthouse fell into such a state of disrepair that the grand jury recommended that the person in charge of the courthouse do a better job of keeping the courthouse closed when it was not in use to prevent the building from becoming sleeping apartments for goats. After attempts to remodel the courthouse to accommodate the growth of the county failed, a new brick courthouse was constructed in 1895.

DUBLIN CITY HALL, 1906–1959. During the Golden Age, city fathers erected a new city hall that would be in keeping with the city's stature. The city officers moved from the old Masonic building at the western end of town to the old Hilton Hotel building on the courthouse square. Rev. George C. Thompson, a local architect, adapted the building for use as city offices and the city fire department, which was organized in 1878. A bell tower was added later. The bell would signal, by the number of rings, the quadrant of the city in which a fire was occurring. The building, located at 107 East Jackson Street, was razed to make room for a county parking lot.

THE DUBLIN POST OFFICE. In 1912, following an intense debate on its location, Dublin's first Federal Building was built on the southwest corner of East Madison and South Franklin Streets, replacing the old building a block to the southwest. This building, designed by James Knox Taylor, features Flemish-bond brickwork designed to increase its strength. Too small from the beginning, the post office was replaced in 1936 by a larger building on the courthouse square, reportedly to handle the increase in the volume of moonshining cases in the Dublin division of the federal court.

THE GREAT FIRE OF 1889. In the pre-dawn hours of May 24, 1889, a spark arose near the intersection of South Lawrence (Laurens) Street and West Jackson Street. Fanned by high winds, the flames spread eastward wiping out 13 buildings and an entire city block, with the exception of Dr. R.H. Hightower's brick building, shown in the upper left corner. Notice the homes in the upper right corner where businesses would soon follow.

A SURVIVOR OF THE GREAT FIRE. Shown here after the Great Fire of 1889 is the store building of Dupree and Bishop, located in the middle of the north side of the 100 block of West Jackson Street. The store building was later moved to South Lawrence Street, just below the present drive-in location of the Bank of Dudley.

THE BUSINESS SECTION OF DUBLIN. This 1911 photograph shows the southwest corner of the courthouse square and a portion of business houses along Dublin's busiest street, West Jackson Street.

GOING TO COURT. Court times were among the busiest days in Dublin. This photograph shows a group of men coming up the walk into the courthouse. West Jackson Street is in the background.

A Bird's-Eye View of Dublin. This 1900 photograph taken from the tower of the courthouse looking east along East Jackson Street shows how many homes were located in the downtown area. In the lower right corner of the image is the Laurens County Courthouse of 1845–1895, which was moved to the corner of South Franklin and East Jackson Streets in 1895.

Another Bird's-Eye View of Dublin. This 1900 photograph taken from the tower of the courthouse looking west along West Jackson Street shows Dublin during a slow time. Along the horizon is the old brick water tower, which stood behind the present-day city hall. Just right of center is the First Methodist Church.

14

THE INTERIOR OF THE SCHAUFELE BUILDING. This 1907 photograph shows the interior of Schaufele's Men's Store. Notice the hats on the front counter that appear to be hovering in mid-air.

THE W.F. SCHAUFELE BUILDINGS. W.F. Schaufele came to Dublin in the mid-1890s and established one of the leading men's fashions stores in Dublin at 210 and 212 West Jackson Street. The two-story building on the left burned in 1912. It was rebuilt and is today occupied by Thompson and Thompson Law Offices.

WEST JACKSON STREET, C. 1914. This photograph looking east shows the northern side of the 100 block of West Jackson Street. The largest building on the left is the Corker Building. The large store in the middle is the Sam Weischelbaum Company, one of Dublin's largest department stores. The building in the center is the R.C. Henry Building, named for riverboat captain R.C. Henry. The courthouse is visible on the right.

WEST JACKSON STREET, C. 1914. This photograph looking west shows the northern side of the 100 block of West Jackson Street. The large store in the middle is the Sam Weischelbaum Company, one of Dublin's largest department stores. The building on the right is the R.C. Henry Building.

THE C.W. BRANTLEY BUILDING, C. 1914. Known to many Dubliners as the old Lovett & Tharpe Building, this three-story building at 201 West Jackson Street was once the tallest building in Dublin. The building, which was built by Dublin banker and businessman, C.W. Brantley in 1904, was home to businesses like the Oconee Pharmacy, J.R. Baggett & Son, and the Shewmake-Hall Company. The middle floor was home to many of Dublin's professional men and the Lyric Theatre. The lodges of the Elk's Club and the Laurens Lodge No. 75, F. & A.M. were located on the top floor.

THE FRED ROBERTS HOTEL. Dublin's premier hotel, a project of the Dublin Chamber of Commerce, was completed in 1926. Fred Roberts was the chairman of the DCC committee during the construction of the building, but he died before it was completed.

THE GREAT SNOWFALL OF 1914. On February 25, 1914, 3 or more inches of snow fell on Dublin. Large snowfalls occurred only about every 20 years during this era. Photographer Doyle Knight took this photograph from one of the upper floors of the First National Bank Building looking north toward the courthouse.

EAST MADISON STREET. The foreground of this 1913 picture shows the recently completed post office and Federal Building. At the extreme right of the picture is the First National Bank, which was nearing completion.

SOUTH JEFFERSON STREET. This 1914 photograph shows the west side of the 100 block of South Jefferson Street looking south. From left to right are the Four Seasons Building, the Taylor-Coleman Pharmacy, the Courier Herald, the Jackson Stores (including a bowling alley), the H.V. Westbrook Department Store, and the Stubbs-Leitch Building.

SOUTH JEFFERSON STREET. This photograph, taken from the just below the railroad on South Jefferson Street, shows the First National Bank Building on the left and the New Dublin Hotel on the right. On the far right of the photograph is the depot of the Macon, Dublin, & Savannah Railroad. Notice the horse-drawn carriage, Dublin's earliest cab, waiting for a passenger at the depot.

19

THE D.D. CUMMINGS BUILDING. Situated at the southeast corner of West Madison Street and South Lawrence Street, at the intersection known as Five Points, is the D.D. Cummings Building. In the early 1900s, Cummings, a former slave, built this building, which was the center of the African-American Business trade in downtown Dublin for most of the 20th century.

SOUTH JEFFERSON STREET, C. 1914. This photograph captures a time when horse-drawn carriages and horse-less carriages shared Dublin's streets.

THE NEW DUBLIN HOTEL. The New Dublin Hotel, built around 1900, was Dublin's top hotel during the Golden Era. Located at 201 South Jefferson Street, the New Dublin Hotel was also home to businesses like the Crescent Pharmacy and Hamlet's Barber Shop. The dining room hosted many of Dublin's business and social gatherings for nearly three decades. The hotel expanded to include the building to the rear and the upper floor of the Burch Building. It was razed in the 1960s for the construction of the Western Auto Store.

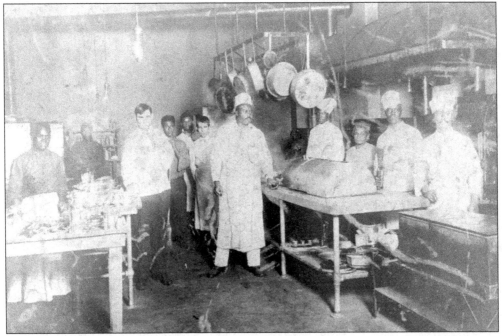

THE KITCHEN OF THE NEW DUBLIN HOTEL. The New Dublin Hotel was opened in 1900 under the management of Thomas Hooks. The hotel's kitchen staff cooked for the hotel guests as well as for many people who came to the hotel to attend meetings.

THE FOUR SEASONS DEPARTMENT STORE. J.E. Smith Jr. opened the largest store in this part of the state in 1904. The Four Seasons Store, managed by E.D. White and R.M. Arnau, boasted that it was only the third department store in the state to have a four-full-page newspaper ad. The capital assets of the store were valued in excess of $100,000. Thousands of people showed up outside the store to see Buster Brown and his dog Tige in February 1907. The company's first store was located in the building now occupied by the Courier Herald at 115 South Jefferson Street.

THE SECOND FOUR SEASONS STORE. In 1910, the Four Seasons moved across the street into a new three-story building built especially for the store and designed by local architect R.B. McGecken. The Four Seasons, modeled after big city stores, carried an inventory of $100,000 in shoes alone. When the county began to go into a depression in 1915, the once-grand store was forced into bankruptcy. The building burned in the early 1970s, but at least the exterior walls of the first floor were saved. During the years between the World Wars, the National Guard had its headquarters in the building.

THE OGBURN BUGGY CO. This two-story building, owned by W.O. Ogburn, was located on East Madison Street. It was sold to Cecil E. Carroll, who converted it to a cotton warehouse.

TOM DANIEL AND SON. Daniel, a Studebaker Automobile dealer, is shown in his garage with his son, G.T. Daniel. Daniel, a skilled mechanic, built his own homemade automobiles.

THE KNIGHTON-FLANDERS DRUG STORE. The drug store of H.W. Knighton and J.T. Flanders was opened in 1912, in the old Anderson Grocery Company building. During the pinnacle of Dublin's prosperity, Dublin was home to more than a half-dozen drug stores.

THE INTERIOR OF PAGE-WALKER DRUG COMPANY. This early 1900s photograph shows the interior of the drug store of Drs. J.M. Page and Sidney Walker. Their store was located on the first floor of the C.W. Brantley Building on the northwest corner of West Jackson and North Lawrence Streets.

Reuben Smith and His Bread Wagon. Reuben Smith is shown in this 1920 photograph standing outside what may have been the store building of Sam Barron on Jackson Street.

West Jackson Street. This 1911 photograph, taken from Monroe Street looking east toward the courthouse, shows Dublin's new sidewalks. On the right of the photograph is the Crystal Theatre, Dublin's premier theater during its Golden Era, and the Robinson Hardware Company, Dublin's largest hardware business.

THE DUBLIN BUGGY COMPANY. Dublin's largest buggy manufacturing company was located on North Jackson Street on the north side of the courthouse square from 1905 to 1911. The building in this photograph was erected in 1911. Unfortunately, because of the increased use of the automobile, buggy manufacturing declined and the business closed. It still stands and is located at 125 East Jackson Street.

THE NORTH SIDE OF THE COURTHOUSE SQUARE, C. 1914. Shown in this photograph, from left to right, are the horse and mule stables of H.H. Smith, Dublin City Hall, T.H. Smith's Sale Stables, and the Dublin Buggy and Wagon Company. At one time, nearly all of the businesses on the courthouse square were related to the horse, mule, and buggy trade.

OUTLER, ARNAU, OUTLER. J.M. Outler, R.M. Arnau, and W.B. Outler operated one of Dublin's leading dry goods and general merchandise stores in Dublin. In 1902, the only long-distance pay phone in Dublin was moved from Herman Hesse's barbershop to their store, which was located in the Henry Building on West Jackson Street.

THE SOUTHLAND VENEER MILL. Located on the site of the River Walk Park on the Oconee River, the Southland Veneer Mill was constructed in 1909 on the site of the Simmons Veneer Mill, which had burned. The mill became known as the Georgia Plywood Company, which operated on the site for nearly five decades.

CLAYTON D. DUDLEY'S STORE. The East Jackson Street store of C.D. Dudley was established in the early 1900s. Dudley and his wife, Katie, along with their son, H.H. "Hub" Dudley, and his wife, Mayme Ford Dudley, developed the largest and most successful group of African-American businesses in Dublin. The building, located at 617 East Jackson Street, is today occupied by Dudley Funeral Home.

THE E.S. STREET FORD BUILDING. This two-story building housed the Ford dealership of E.S. Street. The building, located at the northwest corner of the courthouse square, featured an upstairs garage in which Drs. E.B. Claxon and H. Montford used an elevator to lift their patients, and the patient's car, up to the second floor.

HOBBS & HOBBS GROCERY. This photograph, taken about 1920, shows a typical grocery store of the period. The store, owned by James D. Hall, featured natty displays of groceries. Notice the pyramid stacks of cans along the top shelves.

NORTH JEFFERSON STREET. North Jefferson Street, as shown in this 1913 photograph, was once lined with trees and residences, in stark contrast to the commercial buildings on the street today.

TELEPHONE COMPANY FRAME AND BATTERY ROOM. The men who maintained the operation of the telephones in Dublin are shown in this photograph. Phones were luxuries for most the first half of the 20th century. Direct dialing and direct long-distance service came to Dublin in the 1950s and 1960s, respectively.

THE TELEPHONE AND TELEGRAPH COMPANY. This photograph shows the staff of the joint office of the Southern Bell Telephone Company and the Western Union Telegraph Company on East Madison Street. In the days before radio, play-by-play accounts of the World Series were instantly sent over telegraph lines and diagramed on a chalk board in the telegraph company office for baseball fans.

DUBLIN'S COCA-COLA FOUNDERS. Charles and Harmon Holmes are shown in this photograph standing in front of their Coca-Cola truck. Other members of the Holmes family founded several Coca-Cola Bottling Companies over the state of Georgia.

THE DUBLIN COCA-COLA BOTTLING COMPANY. The Dublin Coca-Cola Bottling Company was incorporated in 1912 by J.W. Geeslin. This building may have been located on Harrison Street, between South Franklin and South Washington Streets.

THE FIRST NATIONAL BANK. Dublin's skyscraper, still known as the tallest building between Macon and Savannah, was completed in 1913 under the leadership of bank president Frank G. Corker. The building, which contained six floors and a foundation to support three additional floors, was designed by Atlanta architect A. Ten Eyck Brown, who designed many buildings in Atlanta, including the Fulton County Courthouse and the Federal Reserve building. Above the bank were 60 offices for Dublin professionals, including Dr. G.R. Lee, who opened his dentistry practice in 1919 and practiced in the building for all or parts of seven decades.

FIRST NATIONAL BANK OFFICERS AND DIRECTORS. This photograph shows the officers and directors of the First National Bank just after the bank moved to its South Jefferson Street skyscraper. The main room of the bank featured a mezzanine above the ground floor. Included in the photograph are W.B. Rice, W.S. Phillips, and A.W. Garrett.

THE CITY NATIONAL BANK. Originally founded as the Citizens Bank in 1902 by E.P. Rentz, this impressive stone building, designed by local architect Rev. George C. Thompson and built by local builder E.J. Fuller, became the City National Bank in 1906. J.E. Smith Jr. organized the "largest bank between Macon and Savannah" under the National Bank system. The national bank notes from the bank are known to be among the rarest notes in the country. Today the building at 109 South Jefferson Street is occupied by attorneys Bill Tribble and Charles Butler.

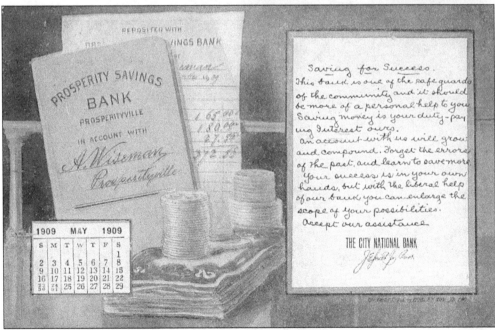

AN EARLY DUBLIN CALENDAR. Each month the City National Bank issued new calendar postcards featuring sound banking advice to their customers. This photograph shows the card for May 1909.

DUBLIN'S FIRST BANK. The Dublin Banking Company, which began as a private bank in 1892, was chartered in February 1899. The bank occupied the corner of the first floor of the R.C. Henry Building at 101 West Jackson Street. Riverboat captain R.C. Henry was the founding president. James M. Finn, recognized as Dublin's "Number One Citizen," was the bank's cashier. The interior of the bank included elaborate marble and pressed-metal ceilings. Notice the spittoons that were strategically placed around the floor.

THE OLD BRICK WATER TOWER. The City of Dublin erected its first water tower about 1898. The imposing structure dominated the western skyline of the town until it was torn down in 1962. It was situated to the rear of the current post office.

DUBLIN'S FIRST CHARTERED BANK. The Laurens Banking Company was chartered in 1898 under the presidency of Hardy Hamilton Smith. The bank was headquartered on the corner of the Leitch-Stubbs Building at 100 West Jackson Street. Various stores and professional offices were also located in the building. The upper floor contained a large meeting hall, which was used for mass meetings, lodge meetings, and a drill hall for the local volunteer militia (the Dublin Guards) during the Spanish-American War.

THE NORTH SIDE OF COURTHOUSE SQUARE. This 1900 photograph shows the northern side of the courthouse square. On the left is the Hilton Hotel, so named for its owner, Attys Hilton. It may have been the first Hilton Hotel in America. In the center may have been a building occupied by photographer J.N. Smith. On the right are the mule and horse stables of Brown and Phillips.

THE CENTER OF DOWNTOWN DUBLIN. These two corners at the western intersection of Jackson and Jefferson Streets were the choice corners for business locations in Dublin. This early 1900 photograph shows the Laurens Banking Company in the Leitch-Stubbs Building and the Dublin Banking Company in the R.C. Henry Building.

THE COURTHOUSE SQUARE. The courthouse square was the scene of outdoor concerts and political speeches for many decades. In the early decades of the 20th century, the square was lined with a short hedge of boxwoods.

THE HICKS BUILDING. This 1895 building, which was owned by the Hicks family, was home to many stores during the Golden Era. The Hick's Drug Store occupied the corner building for several decades. It was at this location on May 7, 1865, when Postmaster John Regan of the Confederate States obtained directions from Freeman Rowe on which road he and the rest of his party, including President and Mrs. Jefferson Davis, should travel in order to escape the Federal cavalry that was one day behind them. The upper floor of the building was used for professional offices.

THE EMERALD CITY BUILDING. Mrs. R.H. Hightower built this building at 110 W. Jackson Street in the early 1900s. It originally housed a drug store and a soda shop and joined the Crystal Theatre with a common doorway. Today the structure is occupied by the Peppercorn Restaurant.

DUBLIN'S FIRST HOSPITAL. Doctors H.T. and C.A. Hodges opened their sanitarium in the J.E. Smith Jr. House at 117 North Franklin Street in 1910.

THE BURCH BUILDING. Dan Burch constructed this three-story building on East Madison Street in 1912 between the then-new post office to the east and the New Dublin Hotel to the west. The building has served as a hospital, hotel, high school, and various stores and professional offices.

THE C.H. KITTRELL BUILDING.
Dr. C.H. Kittrell erected this
quaint-looking building on South
Jefferson Street adjoining the
First National Bank building.
It features a mezzanine above
the first floor and elaborate
pressed metal ceiling.

THE DUBLIN COTTON MILL. One of the largest buildings in Dublin was constructed on Marion Street west of Kellam Road in 1901. The cotton mill, which fell victim to economic crises, went through a series of owners and burned in 1914. A small town, called West Dublin by some, grew up around the mill and included many homes, stores, a Baptist church, and a Methodist church.

THE **R.F. DEESE HOUSE.** The home of R.F. Deese, located at 210 South Calhoun Street, was built in the early 1900s by Dublin's leading furniture merchant. Deese, who came to Dublin in 1895, established his furniture store in 1899 and boasted that it was the largest store between the cities of Macon and Savannah.

THE **PATTILLO HOUSE.** Mr. and Mrs. W.B. Pattillo opened this boarding house on January 1, 1905, in the old H.A. Knight House at 111 East Gaines Street.

The Joseph Daniel Smith House. Smith, possibly the richest man in Dublin, built this home in 1892 on the northwest corner of North Franklin and East Gaines Streets. The house, one of ten owned by Smith, burned before 1905.

W.W. Robinson's Store. W.W. Robinson, one of Dublin's earliest and most successful hardware dealers, constructed his first store in the middle of the south side of the 200 block of West Jackson Street in the 1890s.

STONEWALL STREET. This photograph, taken looking west between the M.H. Blackshear and E.R. Jordan Houses at the eastern end of Stonewall Street, shows only a few trees along the street, which passes through what was once an orchard. Originally known as Stanley Avenue, the road was renamed Stonewall Street after legendary Confederate general Thomas "Stonewall" Jackson. In the early spring, the street is lined with gardens of dogwoods and azaleas.

SOUTH CALHOUN STREET. This street, seen here from Academy Avenue in 1917, was named for South Carolina "state rights" senator, John C. Calhoun. During Dublin's Golden Age, the street was home to Dublin's upper-middle-class families, including the Deeses, Blackshears, Burches, Hatchers, Simons, Jordans, Baums, Tarpleys, and Mahoneys.

ACADEMY AVENUE. This 1913 photograph, taken by Doyle Knight, looks east from the intersection of South Calhoun Street and Academy Avenue. The house on the far left, known in later years as the R.T. Peacock House, was purchased in 1926 by Thomas Hardwick, the new owner and editor of the *Courier Herald*. Before coming to Dublin, Hardwick was a well-known attorney, congressman, senator, and governor of Georgia. While he was governor, Hardwick appointed Rebecca L. Felton, the country's first woman senator.

THE HARDY SMITH HOUSE. This Southern Gothic-style farmhouse was built in the early 1870s, by Hardy Smith, clerk of the Superior Court. Smith, an amputee veteran of the Civil War, was one of the most beloved men of the Golden Age. Smith donated the land for the Methodist church that adjoins his home on West Gaines Street. Smith served as judge of Ordinary Court and as a division commander of the Georgia UCV. His home is currently being restored as a memorial to the military veterans of Laurens County.

CHARLIE KEENE TAKES A BREAK. Keene, one of Dublin's leading grocers of the period, takes a break before loading the last two sacks of flour into his truck. This photograph appears to have been taken looking east on East Madison Street on the side of the New Dublin Hotel.

BOTTLING WORKS. This turn-of-the-20th-century photograph is believed to have been taken looking west at the Artesian Bottling Works on East Madison Street. The cotton compress is visible in the background.

THE CUPOLA OF THE DUBLIN BANKING
CO. This photograph shows a close-
up view of the cupola that adorned
the corner of the Dublin Banking
Company at 101 West Jackson Street.

DUBLIN'S OLDEST HOME. This home,
which was constructed in 1849
near the corner of Rowe Street and
Academy Avenue by Freeman Rowe,
is said to have been the house where
a meal was cooked for the family of
Confederate president Jefferson Davis
while he was attempting to escape
from the Union cavalry, who were
one day behind him when he came to
Dublin on May 7, 1865.

THE CARNEGIE LIBRARY. Maj. J.B. Duggan led the effort to build a public library in Dublin. His request for funds was accepted by philanthropist Andrew Carnegie, who donated $10,000 for the structure, which was built by John Kelley. The library served the citizens of Dublin and Laurens County from 1904 to 1964. In 1967, a group of concerned citizens banded together to save the building from destruction and, in doing so, formed the Laurens County Historical Society, which is now headquartered in the building.

THE D.S. BRANDON HOUSE. D.S. Brandon built this lovely home in the early 1900s. It later became the home of the BPOE Elk's Lodge.

THE OLD COURTHOUSE. This photograph shows workers putting a coat of paint on Laurens County's courthouse. Notice the detailed brick and marble works that once adorned this beautiful building.

THE OLD JAIL. Laurens County's old brick jail was built in 1905. This fortress-like building was located just off the southeast corner of the courthouse square where a county parking lot now lies. The building was designed by Rev. George C. Thompson.

THE HILTON HOTEL. Dublin's premier hotel of the 1890s was known as the Central Hotel, the Hooks House, and the Hilton Hotel. The latter name came from its owner, Attys P. Hilton. It may have been the first Hilton Hotel in America.

THE MARSHALL-PEACOCK CO. The new model cars are proudly displayed in front of the dealership's building, which is still located on the northwest corner of the courthouse square between two parking lots. Before the E.S. Street building on the left was completed, two signs advertising H.H. Smith's Mule Co., the former tenant of the building, and Snowdrift Shortening, manufactured in Dublin by the Empire Cotton Oil Co., were painted on the side of the building. Main Street Dublin and the historical society maintain these signs today.

Two

BELLEVUE AVENUE

THE GRAND HOMES OF BELLEVUE. These mansions, some of them known as catalog houses because they were manufactured and shipped to Dublin in pieces and then assembled on the lot, were the homes of Dublin's leading merchants and businessmen. From left to right are the homes of A.W. Garrett, B.H. Rawls, S.J. Fuller, T.H. Smith, and Stephen Lord.

THE DR. J.M. PAGE HOUSE. This classic 11-room house at 711 Bellevue was built by Dublin attorney T.L. Griner, *c.* 1903. Dr. J.M. Page purchased the house and moved his medical practice to Dublin in 1905. The house was the only one of its kind in this area of the state to feature a ballroom, which was the scene of numerous weddings and social affairs. The house was recently remodeled in 1998 by Kelly and Janice Canady, who operate a bed and breakfast known as the Page House.

THE SMITH-RENTZ-CORKER-CURRY-LOVETT HOUSE. Known as "The Crown Jewel" of Bellevue Avenue, this three-story colonial house was built in 1902 by J.D. Smith at a cost of $13,500, which included a number of out buildings. Smith sold the house to railroad baron E.P. Rentz, who in turn sold it to First National Bank president Frank G. Corker. When Corker moved to Atlanta to look after his business interests, the house became the Claxton-Brigham Hospital and, later, the home of Dublin realtor T.A. Curry Sr. Bill and Jeanelle Lovett made this house their home for six decades. It is now occupied by the family of their son Griffin.

THE **W.W. ROBINSON HOUSE.** This elegant two-story house, located at 501 Bellevue Avenue, was built in 1911 by W.W. Robinson, Dublin's premier hardware merchant and the first president of the Georgia Retail Hardware Dealer's Association. Local architect R.B. McGecken designed the 10-room house, which cost a mere $6,000 to build. It was razed in the mid-1960s to make room for the Firestone Tire Store.

THE **J.R. POWEL HOUSE.** Sitting in a grove of oaks and magnolias, the home of cotton merchant J.R. Powel was built on the site of the home of attorney and railroad baron Col. J.M. Stubbs. When Dr. E.B. Claxton built his hospital on the site in the mid-1930s, he incorporated a portion of the house into his hospital building. In the 1980s, it was the first location of the Dublin Center. The hospital and the house, located at 509 Bellevue Avenue, were razed to make room for a future expansion of the First Baptist Church.

THE IZZIE BASHINSKI HOUSE. Well-known Washington County architect Charles Edward Choate designed the home of cotton merchant and businessman Izzie Bashinski. The Bashinskis were among the several Jewish families who moved to Dublin in the 1890s and 1900s and contributed greatly to the explosive growth of the city during its Golden Era. Bashinski served as mayor of Dublin during World War I and donated his salary to the American Red Cross. The house, built in 1911 and located at 703 Bellevue Avenue, was later purchased by Dr. E.B. and Mrs. Irene Claxton.

THE G.H. WILLIAMS HOUSE. This handsome home, built in the early 1900s, was home to Dublin attorney G.H. Williams. Williams, who practiced law in Dublin for over 50 years, was known as a "Cornfield Lawyer" because of his generosity to some of his clients. Williams served as president of the board of education and was one of Dublin's first historians. Williams was the first to propose the idea of creating Stubbs Park. In 1964, the building at 801 Bellevue Avenue was razed to make room for the Laurens County Library.

THE HARDY HAMILTON SMITH HOUSE. This house was built at 903 Bellevue Avenue around the turn of the 20th century by businessman J.H. Beacham. Beacham sold the house to Smith and moved to Mississippi to engage in the timber business. When the venture failed, Beacham returned to Dublin and, at the request of his family, tried to buy his former home from Smith. Undaunted by Smith's refusal to sell, Beacham bought a lot on the corner at Bellevue Avenue and North Calhoun Street and built a duplicate of his former home, making his wife and children very happy.

THE J.H. BEACHAM HOME. This house was built about 1906 by Dublin businessman J.H. Beacham, whose family wanted a home just like the one they had before they moved to Mississippi. It still stands at 701 Bellevue Avenue.

BELLEVUE AVENUE, C. 1907. This photograph shows Bellevue Avenue in the days before the road was paved. Along the right side of the road, from left to right, are the homes of Dr. J.M. Page, Claude W. Brantley, J.H. Beacham, B.H. Rawls, S.J. Fuller, and T.H. Smith.

BELLEVUE AVENUE. This 1914 photograph shows, from left to right, the homes of Claude W. Brantley, J.R. Broadhurst, and Izzie Bashisnki.

ANGUS D. ALSUP HOUSE. This home was built by Dublin grocer Agnus D. Alsup during the second decade of the 20th century. The house, which is located at 1701 Bellevue Road, is surrounded by gigantic live oaks that are said to have been grown from seedlings brought to Dublin from Wormsloe Plantation near Savannah.

THE JOHN S. AND AUGUSTA STANLEY ADAMS HOME. This home was built around 1900 by John M. Simmons. Mr. and Mrs. Adams moved into the home in 1906. Judge Adams served as an attorney, mayor of Dublin, judge of City Court, and attorney for the Treasury Department. Mrs. Adams was a outstanding statewide leader in the Daughters of the American Revolution, Colonial Dames of America, and the Daughters of 1812. The upper portion of the house, which was located at 822 Bellevue Avenue, was removed after a fire.

THE T.H. SMITH HOME. T.H. Smith, a leading banker and businessman, built this colonial-style home at 605 Bellevue in the early 1900s. Mrs. Smith served a chairman of the Red Cross in Dublin during World War I. The house, which was seriously damaged by fire in 1916, was reconstructed and now holds Adams Funeral Home.

THE JAMES B. SANDERS HOUSE. James B. Sanders came to Dublin in the mid-1880s to teach school. Sanders practiced law in Dublin. He built this house, the oldest house still remaining on Bellevue Avenue, in 1885. Sanders served as mayor of Dublin from 1895 to 1896. The house, which was later known as the Peacock House, is located at 901 Bellevue Avenue. It is now occupied by Hilbun and Helton, Attorneys.

THE THOMAS J. PRITCHETT HOUSE. Pritchett, a timber and naval stores dealer, moved to Dublin in the 1890s. This beautiful house was built around the turn of the 20th century by Pritchett, who founded the Georgia Warehouse and Compress Company. The house, which is located at 702 Bellevue Avenue, was later the home of E.R. Orr, one of Dublin's most popular and effective mayors during the period.

THE ANDREW W. GARRETT HOUSE. Garrett, a top banker and insurance agent of the Golden Era, lived in this colonial home, located at 613 Bellevue Avenue and built by Dublin's premier builder, John Kelley, in 1910.

THE D.W. GILBERT HOUSE. Gilbert, a leading hardware dealer of the period, lived in this early-20th-century home at 714 Bellevue Avenue. Today it is the office of Dr. Lee Whitaker, who has preserved and maintained the beautiful home.

THE JAMES M. FINN HOUSE. Dublin's "Number One Citizen," James M. Finn, built this elegant home at 618 Bellevue, just before the turn of the 20th century.

Three

TRANSPORTATION

ENGINE NO. 99. The entire economy of Dublin and Laurens County once revolved around the railroads. On February 7, 1910, eight trains of over 200 cars were parked at the depot at one time. At the height of the era of trains in Dublin, there were two or more morning trains in and out of Dublin each day.

OUT FOR A RIDE. W.T., Charles, and Henry Stinson took time to pose for this photograph near the rear of the Hicks Building on South Jefferson Street. The structure in the center is the building of the Citizens/City National Bank.

J.D. SMITH & SON. This photograph, taken around 1900, shows a horse-wagon pulling a load of cotton in front of the store of J.D. Smith on the middle of the north side of the courthouse square.

THE WIEUCA. Dr. Ovid Cheek entertained his family and friends on his pleasure boat, the *Wieuca*, for many decades in the first half of the 20th century.

DR. E.B. CLAXTON AND IRIS CLAXTON. One of Dublin's leading physicians is shown taking a spin in his first automobile with his daughter Iris. Dr. Claxton established his first hospital in the Street Building on the northwest corner of the courthouse square in the 1920s and built a modern hospital on Bellevue Avenue in the 1930s on the site of the old John M. Stubbs place.

DUBLIN'S DEPOTS. This retouched photograph shows the South Jefferson Street depots of the Macon, Dublin, & Savannah Railroad on the left, and the Wrightsville & Tennille Railroad on the right. Postcard artists often added clouds and took out distractions such as utility lines, which should be visible here between the poles. Passengers arriving at the depot could take a ride in the buggies positioned in front of the depot.

THE WRIGHTSVILLE & TENNILLE RAILROAD DEPOT. Shown in this photograph is the second depot of the Wrightsville & Tennille Railroad, which was constructed around 1900, remodeled in 1906, and had a second story added in 1911. The depot, located at the northeastern intersection of Martin Luther King Jr. Drive and South Jefferson Street, burned in March 1989, just three days after plans were announced to restore it by Dublin-Laurens Clean and Beautiful.

A Locomotive Crossing the Oconee. This unusual photograph shows a locomotive crossing the Oconee River during a flood, possibly in the winter or spring of 1914.

Dublin's Depots. The single greatest factor in the growth of Dublin during its Golden Era was the location of five railroads that intersected on South Jefferson Street. The depot of the Wrightsville & Tennille Railroad, which also served the Brewton & Pineora, the Dublin & Southwestern, and the Oconee & Western is shown in the upper center of the photograph, while the depot of the Macon, Dublin, & Savannah Railroad is shown in the lower center.

THE RAILROAD BRIDGE. This railroad bridge, shown during a flood, was constructed in 1891 and gave Dublin its first access to rail traffic.

THE DEPOT OF THE MD&S RAILROAD. The Macon, Dublin, & Savannah Railroad, which came to Dublin in the summer of 1891, erected a depot on the east side of South Jefferson Street, north of the railroad in 1902. The building was torn down in the early 1960s.

A Freight Boat on the Oconee. A freight boat fights to move up river during a flood.

A Freight Boat on the Oconee. This freight boat is shown moored to the railroad bridge over Oconee at the wharf of the Wrightsville & Tennille Railroad.

THE OCONEE RIVER. This serene view of the Oconee River, Dublin's lifeblood and the driving force in its rebirth in the late 1800s, was taken from the current site of the River Walk Park, looking north. It was at or near this spot that Confederate president Jefferson Davis crossed the river into Dublin during his attempted escape to freedom on May 7, 1865.

THE OCONEE RIVER BRIDGE, 1891–1920. This simple but sufficient bridge was the first to permanently span the Oconee River. The railroad river bridge can be seen in the background. This photograph, c. 1913, was taken from the present site of the River Walk Park, looking south.

THE FIRST DUBLIN BRIDGE. Dublin's first permanent passenger bridge over the Oconee River, completed in 1891, is shown here in a 1914 photograph during a flood. The center section of the bridge sat on a pivot, allowing it to swing around to open the bridge for river boat traffic.

THE SECOND RIVER BRIDGE. In 1920, the Laurens County Commission funded a second river bridge to replace the first bridge, which was constructed in 1891. The bridge was replaced in 1953 with the W.H. Lovett Bridge.

THE NEW DUBLIN AND THE LOUISA. The pride of Dublin's fleet of river boats are shown together in this photograph, which was taken prior to 1912. It was in April of 1912, when the *Titanic* sunk in the Atlantic Ocean, that passengers were banned from pleasure cruises aboard the river steamers. The *New Dublin* is shown in the rear with its passengers on her bow and the *Louisa* is shown in the front. Notice the straight-backed deck chairs on the boats.

OLD NO. 40. This Baldwin locomotive was the No. 40 train of the Wrightsville & Tennille Railroad. It was put into service in the early 1900s. Shown in this photograph are, from left to right, A.T. Cochran, engineer; Lawson Stephens, fireman; Grif Jackson, brakeman, and J.C. Hamilton, conductor.

Four

OUR CHURCHES

THE FIRST BAPTIST CHURCH. Architect Alexander Blair modeled this magnificent building after Melrose Abbey in Scotland. The building, located at the northwest corner of North Church Street and Bellevue Avenue, was completed in 1907. The church congregation is Dublin's oldest, going back to the year 1826.

Mrs. W.A. Talliaferro's Sunday School Class. This First Baptist Church Sunday school class was started in 1911 by the preacher's wife, Mrs. Talliaferro. In one year, the class grew from one dozen to nearly ten dozen members. Notice the obligatory dog, which often wandered into early-20th-century group photographs just in time to have its picture taken.

The First Baptist Church. Dublin's Baptists built their second church building on the northwest corner of North Church Street and Bellevue Avenue in the mid-1850s. It was removed to North Decatur Street in the early 1900s and given to the congregation of the Second A.B. or Scottsville Baptist Church.

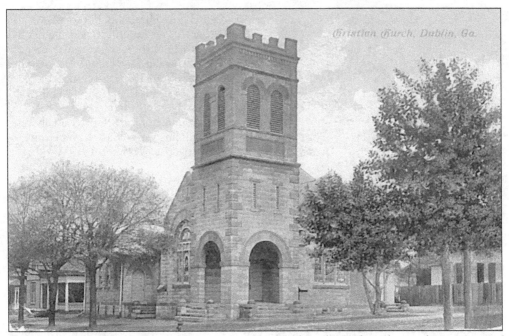

THE FIRST CHRISTIAN CHURCH. This quaint stone building, located on the northeast corner of North Jefferson and East Gaines Streets, was built in 1908, ten years after the First Christian Church was organized.

THE LADIES AID SOCIETY. This 1920 photograph shows the ladies of the First Christian Church on the front steps of the church.

THE HENRY MEMORIAL PRESBYTERIAN CHURCH. This beautiful wooden church was located at the southeastern corner of North Jefferson Street and East Columbia Street. Built in 1899, the church was named for Capt. R.C. Henry, Dublin's leading riverboat captain in the 1880s and a founder of the Presbyterian church. The building was sold to the Jefferson Street Baptist Church in 1919.

THE HENRY MEMORIAL PRESBYTERIAN CHURCH. This church building was constructed on Bellevue Avenue in 1920 under the leadership of Dr. J.G. Patten, who was beloved by members of all denominations in Dublin.

72

THE FIRST METHODIST CHURCH. Rev. George C. Thompson, who moonlighted as an architect, designed the new church building, which featured a tall roof with a spiral steeple in the front center. Thompson incorporated European-style buttresses to support the roof. Another unique feature was the rope-shaped bricks, which lined the stained-glass windows. Rev. M.A. Morgan conducted the first services in the new sanctuary in 1894.

First Methodist Church, Dublin, Ga.

THE FIRST METHODIST CHURCH. In 1910, the members of the church remodeled the building, eliminating the steeple. The church was used for a variety of community meetings. In 1899, 1919, and 1937, the delegates of the South Georgia Conference met in the church for their annual conference. Rev. George Thompson, the original architect and a former pastor of the church, designed the changes.

THE CATHOLIC CHURCH OF THE IMMACULATE CONCEPTION. The Catholics of Dublin, with the aid of Mrs. Victoire Stubbs and Msgr. George Duvall, built their church in 1910. John Kelly constructed the building according to the plans of architect Frank Seeburg of Philadelphia. The first mass was held on June 25, 1911, under the direction of Bishop Benjamin Keiley.

CHRIST EPISCOPAL CHURCH. Dublin's Episcopalians completed this beautiful wooden church, Dublin's oldest, on a lot on Academy Avenue donated by Dr. R.H. Hightower. The building was consecrated on February 5, 1899, by Bishop Nelson. The church features a cross, or cruciform, design, and the interior ceiling is reminiscent of the bottom of an ark, symbolizing that the Church is the ark of the children of God.

THE FIRST AFRICAN BAPTIST CHURCH. Dublin's first church for former slaves was established in 1867 on the western edge of the town commons. This building, located at the corner of Telfair and Church Streets, was built in 1914. One of the church's early leaders was Rev. Norman McCall, whose funeral procession in 1904 was said to have been nearly 2 miles long.

THE ST. PAUL AME CHURCH. This church, originally known as Brown's Chapel AME Church, was established in 1878. The construction of the building in this photograph was started in 1903 and was not fully completed until 1917. The church was the focal point of a small community of African Americans who lived in the area.

JACKSON CHAPEL, CME CHURCH. This church was built in the Scottsville neighborhood of northeastern Dublin around the turn of the 20th century. It is located on East Gaines Street.

THE LADIES AID SOCIETY. This 1904 photograph shows the ladies of the Ladies Aid Society of the First Baptist Church. The group is shown standing on the front steps of the old wooden Baptist church that stood on the corner of North Church Street and Bellevue Avenue for most of the last half of the 19th century.

Five

OUR SCHOOLS

DUBLIN HIGH SCHOOL. This two-story building, now Dublin City Hall, was constructed in 1902 at a cost of $25,000. It contained 12 classrooms and an 860-seat auditorium that was the site of many of the major civic and cultural events in Dublin for nearly eight decades, including the first years of the St. Patrick's Festival. It later became known as Central Elementary before being remodeled in 1959 for use as the city hall. The building, which occupied the site of Dublin's earliest schools, was designed by Rev. George C. Thompson of Dublin.

THE TELFAIR STREET SCHOOL. A group of boys pose outside of the Telfair Street School, which was established in the years after World War I under the direction of its principal, Susie W. Dasher, one of Dublin's most outstanding educators. The school was located in what is now a city park bordered by Flanders and Pritchett Streets.

DUBLIN ACADEMY. Dublin Academy was opened in 1890 on a lot between the swimming pool of the present-day Elk's Club on Academy Avenue and Palmer Street. It served as the school for white students until January 20, 1901, when it was burned by school janitor Robert Wells.

SAXON HEIGHTS SCHOOL. Located on the corner of Smith and Saxon Streets, this two-story wooden school building, designed by local minister George C. Thompson, was built in 1908. It was a near duplicate of Johnson Street School and was located in a neighborhood that was called "Quality Hill." The structure was used until a brick school was constructed in the mid-20th century.

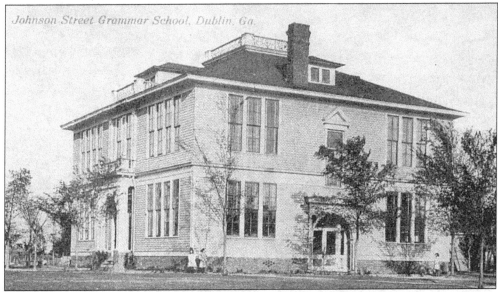

THE JOHNSON STREET SCHOOL. Dublin's first solely exclusive elementary school opened in the fall term of 1905. When no architect made a bid on the design, the building committee selected local architect and minister George C. Thompson to design the two-story wooden building, which was located on the southeast corner of North Franklin and East Johnson Streets and was used until the middle of the 20th century. The building featured a fire escape in the form of a slide, which was the favorite place to play during off days from school.

THE 1916-1917 DUBLIN HIGH BASKETBALL TEAM. Dublin's boys team finished the season with a 6-1 record, including a 28-0 shutout of Sandersville. Among those playing for Dublin that year were Burch, Corker, White, and Satterfield.

DUBLIN HIGH'S FIRST FOOTBALL TEAM. The Dublin Irishmen, under the coaching of W.J. Boswell, had a superior season in the school's first year of playing football in 1919. The Dublin team won the inaugural game over Swainsboro, 45-0, and came back to drub the hapless Swainsboro team in a rematch by the score of 86-0, setting a state record at the time.

THE DUBLIN IRISHMEN BASEBALL TEAM OF 1916. This team, one of Dublin High's first, is shown pictured sitting on the front steps of the school.

DOMESTIC SCIENCE CLASS. The 11th-grade domestic art class at Dublin High School is shown here in 1920.

DUBLIN GIRL'S TENNIS TEAM, 1920. Sporting the long dresses worn by women tennis players at the time, this team, known as "The Flying Racquets," was composed of Lula King, Mavis Weddington, Madge Jordan, Mary Lena Martin, Ruth Broadhurst, and Carolyn Summerlin.

**THE CLASS MASCOT OF 1920–
1921.** Billie Blinn was the mascot
for Dublin High School in the
school year of 1920–1921.

THE CLASS MASCOT OF 1919–1920. Lynette
Mahoney was the mascot for Dublin High
School in the school year of 1919–1920.

THE DUBLIN GIRL'S GLEE CLUB. The members of the glee club shown in this 1920 photograph are Lucile Cox, Jennie Lester, and Mattie Mae Anderson (guitars); Mary Thompson, Martha Garrett, and Gladys Wynne (ukuleles); and Myrtle Sykes, Florence Simmons, Elizabeth Chappell, and Saxon Rowe (mandolins).

THE 1920–1921 12TH DISTRICT CHAMPIONS. Dublin's basketball team, "The Green Whirl," won the 12th Congressional District title with a record of 5-2, including a 63-3 victory over Swainsboro and a 31-15 victory over Sale City, the South Georgia champions. Playing on the team were Brigham White, Doyle Sconyers, Tom Harville, Emory Daniels, Walter Jackson, Victor Slater, and Broadus Martin.

Six

LIFE IN THE
EMERALD CITY

GOING FOR A RIDE. Henry Hicks is shown here in 1898 pulling his brother Charles in a goat cart.

A BIRTHDAY PARTY. This party took place on July 16, 1911, at the home of Thomas Hardy Smith and Lucy Twitty Smith (the lady standing on the porch). The home was remodeled into the present-day Adams Funeral Home on Bellevue Avenue.

POPE'S MILL AND GIN. This photograph, taken around 1912, shows a typical day at the cotton gin on East Madison Street in the late summer and early fall in Dublin. Farmers from all areas of the county brought their crop into town. In 1911, Laurens County produced over 60,000 bales of cotton weighing 500 pounds each.

THE GEORGIA STATE CONFEDERATE REUNION, 1920. In May 1920 those remaining Confederate veterans from Georgia who could travel gathered in Dublin for the state reunion. This photograph, taken from the Schaufele Building at 210 West Jackson Street, shows a big parade at the time. The courthouse is visible on the far right.

THE CONFEDERATE MONUMENT. A monument to the soldiers from Laurens County who fought for the South during the Civil War was dedicated on Confederate Memorial Day in 1912, following a three-year period of bickering and the lack of funds to pay the sculptor. The statue, weighing in at 92,000 pounds, sat under a cover for over three years while the money was raised, one dollar at a time.

THE DUBLIN BAND. The "Pride of Dublin" is shown here in 1910. Director Paul Verpoest's band was among the best in the state of Georgia. The band represented Georgia at the National Confederate Reunions from 1911 to 1914.

A BAND CONCERT ON COURTHOUSE LAWN. The Dublin bands, under the direction of Prof. Paul Verpost and others, were popular attractions for social and political events. For special occasions, bandstands were constructed on the courthouse grounds for the musical presentations.

CAR AND MOTORCYCLE RACES ON BELLEVUE. This 1913 photograph shows the crowds lining Bellevue Avenue trying to catch a glimpse of daring young men in their horse-less carriages and on Indian motorcycles, racing down Bellevue Avenue at speeds of up to 85 miles per hour.

THE FINISH LINE. As the automobile became more popular, the men of Dublin raced their prize cars from the Robinson place on Bellevue Road to the Carnegie Library. The races began in 1911. This photograph, taken between 1912 and 1914, shows the Confederate monument in front of the library.

THE PAVILION AT STUBBS PARK. Stubbs Park was established by the city of Dublin in 1909. The first part of the park was completed in 1910. A pavilion was constructed in the triangular portion of the property that is known as the Grady Wright Park. The huge pines, shown in this 1914 photograph, still stand nearly 90 years later. The houses in the background are situated along Crescent Drive and South Drive.

THE STUBBS MILL BRANCH. This photograph shows the creek that flows through Stubbs Park. Dublin attorney and businessman John M. Stubbs established a large farm surrounding his house on Bellevue Avenue. At the northeastern edge of his farm, Stubbs constructed a grist mill and cotton gin, harnessing the water power of the creek. The area where the mill pond was located became the main area of Stubbs Park in 1910.

STUBBS PARK. This 1914 photograph shows the whitewashed bases of the tall pine trees that still adorn Stubbs Park. Stubbs Park has been the site of political and social gatherings for nine decades. Dublin High's first basketball game was played outdoors in the park. Georgia's secretary of agriculture spoke to a large crowd here in 1915. Georgia's populist leader Sen. Thomas E. Watson, spoke from the stump in the park during the senatorial campaign of 1920, the same year in which Georgia Confederate Veterans held a picnic in the park.

THE STUBBS PARK SWIMMING POOL. This is the earliest known photograph of a swimming pool in Dublin. The pool was located near the present stage in the park and was a favorite summertime spot for Dublin's children.

A Horse-Driven Fire Engine. City fathers were proud of this early 1900s engine, shown parked in front of the city hall. When fire bells rang, citizens would rush to the scene of the fire. One man rushed to the roof to cut a hole in the top of the burning building, completely unaware of the draft he was creating. Critics claimed the motto of the fire department in those days was "We never lose a chimney!"

A July Fourth Parade. A bevy of Dublin's beautiful women and American flags adorn one of Dublin's firetrucks in this 1912 photograph, which was taken in front of the Brantley Building on West Jackson Street.

DUBLIN'S MILITARY LEADERS. Gen. James A. Thomas, a Dublin attorney, a state commander of the Georgia Confederate Veterans, commander of the Army of the Tennessee UCV, and national commander of the United Confederate Veterans from 1925 until his death in 1929, is shown with his son, Col. James Adran Thomas, who was commander of the 121st United States Infantry in World War I. The younger Thomas died aboard his transport ship just before reaching France.

THE FIRST BALE OF COTTON. This photograph, taken outside of a cotton warehouse on Madison Street, shows the first bale of cotton produced by a Laurens County farmer in July 1913. The news of the first cotton bloom and the first bale of cotton ginned in the county became front-page news during the Golden Era.

TOM DANIEL AND HIS CATCH. Tom Daniel stands beside his Studebaker automobile in this 1913 photograph, showing off his string of fish at the Oconee River Boat Yard.

HORSE AND BUGGY. This remarkable photo, taken around 1905, captures a horse looking for a few blades of grass.

ONE OF DUBLIN'S FIRST FOOTBALLERS. Rowe Hicks, shown in the center of this 1903–1904 photograph, played football for Mercer University in Macon. The university experienced a severe problem in fielding a team in 1903, losing their only game, 46-0, to Georgia Tech. The contract with Tech called for a $1,000 forfeiture for failing to play. The Mercer Bears managed to field a team but couldn't find a coach.

95

BATHING BEAUTIES AT TYBEE ISLAND. A group of Dublin women are shown in this photograph taken about 1910. Excursion trips to Tybee Island were popular during the summer months. The trip, which began in the early morning hours and ended in the late evening, could be made for less than $2 on the Wrightsville & Tennille Railroad through its connections with the Central of Georgia, which had its terminus on the beach at Tybee.

HIS FIRST CAR. Haywood Leland Moore is shown at the wheel of his father's Maxwell automobile. Haywood grew up to become a doctor. His father, the Rev. Leland Moore, was a well-known minister and educator in Laurens and surrounding counties.

THE M.B. CARROLL FAMILY. The family of M.B. Carroll is shown in this 1904 photograph on the front steps of their Academy Avenue home. From left to right are Seth M. Carroll, Mack B. Carroll, Clarence W. Carroll, Maude P. Carroll, and Mack B. Carroll Jr. On the tricycle is Cecil E. Carroll, one of Dublin's leading businessmen of the mid-20th century.

DOROTHY BEACHAM AND NURSE. This 1905 photograph shows Dorothy Beacham and her nurse, standing in front of Beachman's Bellevue Avenue home.

THE CONSUMMATE HORSEWOMAN, 1916. Annie Pickens Simons Smith is shown here riding her horse in Stubbs Park near the houses along Crescent Drive.

GOOD FRIENDS, C. 1900. Dr. Hugh McCall Moore, Sam Prince, and a friend take a moment to relax during this studio photo shoot.

Henry Hooks and His Goat. Henry Taylor Hooks, the son of Gabriel Stubbs Hooks and Eugenia Whitaker Hooks, is shown in this 1880s photograph with his pet goat, "Royal Bumper."

James Joseph Flanders. One of Dublin's "Top Cops" during the Golden Era, Flanders also served as sheriff of Laurens County from 1908 to 1914.

THE WORLD WAR I MONUMENT. The United Daughters of the Confederacy raised the funds to establish a monument to those Laurens Countians who died in World War I. A movement is underway to add the names of additional men who lost their lives during the war, but who were inadvertently omitted from the original monument, which is located on the courthouse grounds.

THE DUBLIN GUARDS. During the Spanish-American War, militia units were formed in many Georgia cities. The guards trained in the meeting hall of the Stubbs-Leitch Building on the corner of West Jackson and South Jefferson Streets under the command of Capt. L.Q. Stubbs, a mayor of Dublin, who is shown front and center in this photograph.

SHAKESPEARE IN THE PARK. The Woman's Study Club presented a Shakespeare Tercentenary in Stubbs Park in 1916. Shown here, from left to right, are May Robinson Lawson, Roberta Smith, Josie Cranston, Helen McCall Bashinski, Ruth Hicks Porter, Augusta Stanley Adams, Mrs. Warthen Evans, and Minnie Mae Green Bartlett.

THE OLD CITY CEMETERY. Dublin's oldest existing cemetery dates back to at least the year 1819. Only a portion of the graves of the town's most prosperous individuals have survived. By the early 1900s, the cemetery was full and therefore no longer used for burials. It is located at the rear of the First United Methodist Church on West Gaines Street.

THE NORTHVIEW CEMETERY MAUSOLEUM. In 1904, the city of Dublin established a new city cemetery on North Franklin Street. In 1915, a group of investors led by Frank Corker established a corporation to build and maintain the mausoleum. The venture failed and the building was sold to the city.

LORD INFANT. Infant deaths during the Golden Era were all too common. Many grieving parents spared no expense in gravestones that expressed their sorrow, such as this one on the grave of an infant son of Mr. and Mrs. Stephen Lord that lies in Northview Cemetery.

Scottsville Cemetery. Located on North Decatur Street is the Dublin City Cemetery (Scottsville Cemetery) for African Americans who lived in Dublin in the decades before and after the turn of the 20th century. The cemetery once contained several hundred graves, but now only contains about 15 marked graves.

Dudley Cemetery. Located at the intersection of North Decatur Street is Dudley Cemetery, a private cemetery established by the owners of Dudley Funeral Home. Northeast of the Dudley Cemetery and across Hunger and Hardship Creek is "Cross the Creek" Cemetery, which was established by the city of Dublin in 1911 for its African-American citizens.

SAILOR MAN. Robert Henry "Bob" Hightower III is shown in his brand-new sailor suit. Hightower graduated from Georgia Tech during World War II and entered the U.S. Navy, in which he served for four years as a lieutenant.

SHAVE AND HAIR CUT, TWO BITS. This early 1900s photo of an unknown Dublin barbershop brings back memories to older generations. At the height of Dublin's prosperity, there were over a dozen barbershops in the downtown area.

DOYLE KNIGHT, PHOTOGRAPHER. Doyle Knight took many of the photographs in this book. Though he took thousands of pictures over several decades, most of them have not survived. This photograph was taken of Knight in the Oconee Pharmacy, where he worked.

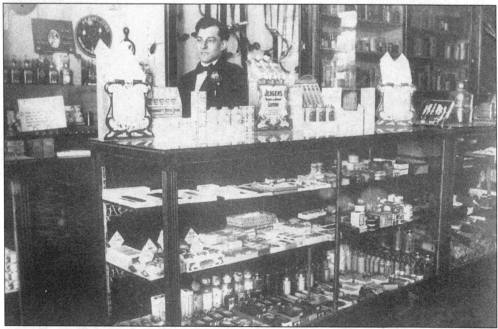

E. ROSS JORDAN. Jordan, owner of the Oconee Pharmacy, is shown here in a photograph taken by his business associate, Doyle Knight. Jordan became involved in the 12th District fairs held in Dublin every fall. For his outstanding work, Jordan was offered and accepted a position with the Georgia state fair. His son Mack donated a large portion of the photographs in this book.

A Boy's Best Friend. While most young boys have dogs or cats for pets, Emanuel Dreyer chose a pet rooster, which he named "Billy," as his best friend.

A Touring Car. Mrs. Olga Buchan goes for a ride in a touring car in this *c.* 1915 photograph.

A Tom Thumb Wedding. This 1914 photograph shows five Dublin children playing in a make-believe wedding. From left to right are Dean Dryer, Sophia Camp, unknown, Elizabeth Burgess, and unknown.

The Children of the Confederacy. A group of youngsters poses in the 1920s, when Dublin was the host to the 14th State Convention of the Children of the Confederacy. The chapter was named for Adelaine Baum, who is shown in the polka-dot dress in the front row. Eugenia Rawls, who left Dublin to star on Broadway and off-Broadway for five decades, is second from the left in the back row.

A Dublin Wedding. Charlie Lou Peacock, Andrew King, and their wedding party are shown here in this 1911 photograph, which was taken at the home of W.L. Joiner on the corner of Rowe and West Madison Streets. From left to right are Fannie King, Marvird Prince, Dena Campbell, W.L. Joiner, Charlie Lou Peacock, unknown, Andrew King, Rev. W.A. Talliaferro, Mrs. W.L. Joiner, Bessie Lee Keen, Sally Walker, Carrie Jane Hicks, and Carl Hilburn.

Telegram! Telegram! Before the days of e-mail, instantaneous electronic mail came in the form a telegraph. The telegrapher would convert the dot and dash signals into words, write it out by hand or in type, and give it to a messenger boy, like the one shown in this photograph of the Western Union Office in Dublin.

A Red Cross Parade. When the local boys began to be sent overseas to fight in World War I, the people of Dublin and Laurens County responded with thousands of dollars in contributions to support the war effort and humanitarian causes in Europe. This 1918 photograph shows a parade held during the height of the war.

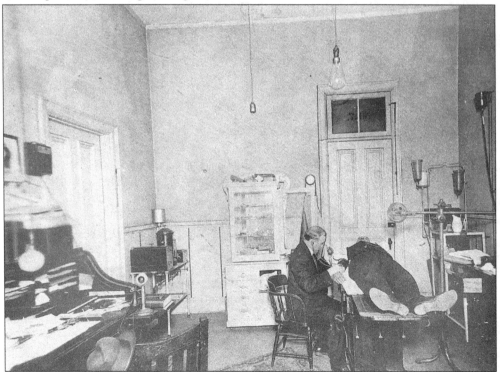

Dr. William C. Thompson's Office. Dr. Thompson, who opened one of Dublin's first hospitals in the old courthouse building, is shown examining one of his patients.

UNCLE R.W. MILLER. Miller, who came to Dublin in 1895, opened a bicycle shop in Dublin and then became the first automobile dealer in Dublin in 1907. He steadfastly believed in the power and the speed of his Cadillac automobiles, and often raced the trains from Tennille to Dublin, winning most of those races. He also operated one of the first bowling alleys in Dublin. A skilled gunsmith and locksmith, he worked at his trade for parts of eight decades in Dublin.

HATTIE BEACHAM. Mrs. Beacham, who founded the Dublin Sash & Door Co. in Dublin in 1920, was one of Dublin's first businesswomen. She is shown here in a 1904 photograph believed to have been taken on Tucker Street.

DUBLIN'S FIRST INNKEEPER. Gabriel Stubbs Hooks came to Dublin in 1884 to operate a shingle mill. In 1886, he took over the management of Dublin's first hotel, the Troup House on South Jefferson Street. He leased the Hilton Hotel on the north side of the courthouse square and operated it under the name of the Hooks House. He is shown here with his wife, Eugenia Adelaide Whitaker Hooks.

THE NEW DUBLIN. The *New Dublin*, a freight-moving steamboat, is shown here in the early 1900s. Before 1907, messages on postcards had to be written on the front and not the back of the card.

A Sunday School Class. This 1898 photograph shows the girl's Sunday school class of the First Baptist Church. Shown in the center is the teacher, Miss Carrie Duncan.

Roberts Buick Co. Dublin auto dealer Fred Roberts operated his Buick dealership in the early 1920s. He died while leading the project to build a new hotel, which was named in his memory.

THE MASONIC LODGE. This two-story building served as the lodge of Laurens Lodge No. 75 F&AM from the mid-1850s until the mid-1890s. The building, which stood on the site of the present-day city hall, was used as a school and a city hall. It was eventually moved to West Gaines Street and converted into a private home.

AN OCONEE RIVER STEAMBOAT. Steamboat traffic in Dublin flourished on the Oconee River from the late 1870s until the early 1910s.

FIVE GIRLS. This quintet of unknown girls posed for this unusual photographby J.N. Smith, Dublin's photographer in the 1890s.

Dr. George Washington Jenkins. Jenkins, a veteran of the Civil War, is shown in his cramped medical office, sitting between the fireplace and the operating/examination table.

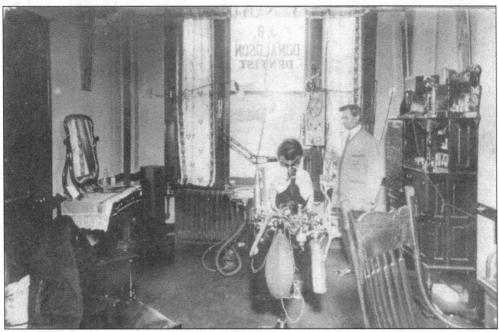

Dr. J.B. Donaldson's Office. This real-photo postcard gives us a glimpse of a turn-of-the-20th-century dental office in Dublin, when going to the dentist was truly a painful experience.

WILLIAM JENNINGS BRYAN. Bryan, who was one of the most popular men in America around the turn of the 20th century, spoke to a large crowd in the Chautauqua Auditorium, on the southwest corner of West Madison and South Monroe Streets, during the Summer Festival of 1911. Bryan was a quadrennial loser in his presidential campaigns.

DR. FREDERICK COOK. At left, Dr. Cook, who falsely claimed to have been the first man to reach the North Pole, spoke to an audience at the 1902 Chautauqua Festival in Dublin. The topic of his speech was "Antarctic Nights," in which he recounted his experiences on man's first trip to the South Pole.

BABY IN A CARRIAGE. This unknown child appears to have posed patiently for the photographer, but appearances can be deceiving. The baby carriage was typical of the period.

THE SOUTHERN EXCHANGE BANK BUILDING. The Southern Exchange Bank was organized to capitalize on the trade of cotton in Dublin during the 1910s. This building, which was erected in 1914 at the northwest corner of South Franklin Street and East Madison Street, was located across the street from the post office and the warehouse of the Georgia Cotton Warehouse and Compress Company.

THE GILBERT HARDWARE CO. D.W. Gilbert built his two-story hardware building at 123 West Jackson Street around 1900. In 1911, the building was used as the site of the first 12th **THE CORKER BUILDING.** Dublin attorney, mayor, and banker Frank G. Corker built this store/office

building at 115 West Jackson Street in 1900.

Seven

LEADERS OF
THE EMERALD CITY

JAMES M. FINN. After four decades of
serving the city of Dublin in numerous
capacities, Finn was named Dublin's
"Number One Citizen." Finn founded
the Telephone Exchange, the Dublin
Banking Company, the Dublin Chamber
of Commerce, the Dublin Cotton Mills,
the Georgia Warehouse and Compress
Company, the Dublin Peanut Co., the
Dublin Stockyards, the Dublin Lumber
Co., the 12th District Fair Assoc., Citizens
Guarantee Insurance Company, Finn-
Garrett-Holcomb Real Estate, the Dublin
Chautauqua Association, the Southland
Veneer Company, and the Dublin Red
Cross. In addition to this, he served as a
director on the board of education, the
Wrightsville & Tennille Railroad, the
Bank of Wrightsville, as chairman of the
World War I Savings Bond Committee, the
Laurens County Centennial Committee,
and as vice president of the Georgia State
Chamber of Commerce.

Dr. Charles H. Kittrell. Dr. Kittrell moved to Dublin at the turn of the 20th century and established his optometry and jewelry store on South Jefferson Street. Kittrell, the leading force in the Chautauqua movement in Dublin, became the first person to manufacture eyeglasses outside of a large city in the Southeast. He was also a leader in education in the city and the county and one of Dublin's most outstanding community leaders.

Katie Dudley. This native of Washington, D.C. came to Dublin in the early 1900s. She married Clayton Dudley and was one of Dublin's premier businesswomen. Mrs. Dudley taught school, and Dublin's first housing project, located on Washington Street, was named Katie Dudley Village in her honor.

WILLIAM PRITCHETT. Pritchett, a leading timber and cotton man in Dublin, is shown here in this 1880s photograph in a military uniform, which may have been the uniform of the Savannah Hussars, a local militia unit.

HARRIS MCCALL STANLEY. Stanley, a member of one of Laurens County's oldest families, began his career in the newspaper business in Dublin. He served as president of the Georgia Press Association, president of the board of education, and as Georgia's first commissioner of commerce and labor from 1912 until 1937. During his term in office, he led the establishment of the Atlanta Farmer's Market.

Dr. R.H. Hightower. Dr. Hightower built the first brick building in Dublin in the 1880s and the only one on the block to survive the fire of 1889. Dr. Hightower built the first bridge, a wooden affair, over the Oconee River, but it washed away during a great flood.

Joseph Daniel Smith. Smith was Dublin's wealthiest man at the turn of the century. He owned nearly half of the buildings on the courthouse square and nearly a dozen dwellings, not to mention thousands of acres of farm and timber land.

JUDGE JOHN THOMAS DUNCAN. As a 21 year old lawyer, Duncan was elected sheriff of Laurens County. Duncan served as clerk of the Superior Court during the Civil War. After the war he served as judge of the Ordinary, now Probate Court, in addition to serving as a state representative. It was Judge John Thomas Duncan who spearheaded the drive to build a bridge over the Oconee River. Undaunted by the voter failure to approve a bond election in 1883, Duncan finally accomplished his quest in 1891. Several days later he collapsed during a court session and died one week later. The building of the bridge over the Oconee was one of the critical factors in Dublin's explosive growth in its Golden Era.

ALBERT R. ARNAU. Arnau was one Dublin's leading bankers and businessmen during the Golden Era. Arnau served as mayor of Dublin and was chosen by Gov. Clifford Walker to be the executive secretary of the state of Georgia in the 1920s.

COL. JOHN M. STUBBS. Stubbs, who served as lieutenant colonel under the command of Stonewall Jackson, came to Dublin in the 1870s to practice law and operate a farm on the edge of the city. His home and farm, known as Liberty Hill, was located on Bellevue Avenue and encompassed a large area along the northern and southern edges of Bellevue, which was then called the Dublin-Hawkinsville Wagon Road. Stubbs led the development of river boat operations and founded the Macon, Dublin, and Savannah Railroad. Stubbs Park was named in his honor, following his death in 1907.

LUCIEN QUINCY STUBBS. Stubbs, son of Col. John M. Stubbs, was easily Dublin's most popular mayor of the 20th century. He was elected on five occasions over a 34-year period. City electric and water lines were installed during his second administration. During his fourth administration, the city first began paving the streets. He died in 1933, while serving as deputy clerk of the Dublin Division of the Federal Court.

E.R. ORR. One of Dublin's most popular mayors, E.R. Orr served two terms in office. During his first term he led the establishment of Northview Cemetery, which was nearly named in his honor. Orr also led the building of the First Baptist Church while all the time managing a large grocery business and a variety of other civic and business affairs. Orr, a rare Republican in the early 20th-century South, was named postmaster of Dublin by President Warren G. Harding in 1922.

LEWIS CLEVELAND POPE. Pope joined the Dublin Guards of the State Militia while in high school. He moved up through the ranks to become captain of the guards. In 1919, Pope was commander of Co. A of the 121st Infantry, which was the first National Guard company commissioned in the southern United States. He served as adjutant general of the Georgia National Guard in the 1920s. Colonel Pope died during World War II while in command of the 121st Infantry stationed at Fort Jackson, South Carolina.

125

REV. WHITEFORD S. RAMSAY.
Dublin's most beloved man of the
late 19th century was Lieutenant
Colonel Ramsay, who served in the
14th Georgia Infantry during the
Civil War. Lieutenant Colonel
Ramsay was one of the youngest
Colonels in the Army. He returned
to Dublin and spent the last 35
years of his life in the ministry,
including over 20 years at the
First Baptist Church. Reverend
Ramsay was the first county school
superintendent. His funeral, held
in 1900, was said to have been the
largest in the history of the county.

J.E. SMITH JR. Smith, known to some
as "Banjo" Smith, was one of the prime
movers and shakers of Dublin. Smith
was involved in all facets of Dublin's
banking, industrial, and business
communities, as well as numerous civic
and cultural organizations.

126

CONGRESSMAN WILLIAM WASHINGTON LARSEN. Larsen, an Emanuel County native, came to Dublin in 1912 to practice law. In 1914, Larsen was appointed to the judgeship of the newly created Dublin Superior Court Judicial Circuit. In 1916, Judge Larsen defeated the powerful Congressman Dudley Hughes and was elected to represent the 12th Congressional District of Georgia for the first of his nine consecutive terms. Congressman Larsen was responsible for the new Federal Building, which was built on the courthouse square in 1936.

DR. CHARLES HICKS. Dr. Hicks, who was elected to the presidency of the Georgia Medical Association, practiced medicine in Dublin from 1884 to 1908. Dr. Hicks was an expert in discovering the causes of malaria in the area and was a member of the state board of health at the time of his death.

Dr. Joseph Morgan Page. Dr. Page came to Dublin in 1903 from Wrightsville. He moved into the home now known as Page House on Bellevue Avenue. Dr. Page founded the Commercial Bank and built many homes and commercial buildings in the city. Dr. Page is shown in this photograph as a senator representing Laurens County in the Georgia Senate.

Andrew W. Garrett. Garrett came to Dublin in the early 1890s and was a leading banker, civic leader, and businessman for nearly 40 years. Garrett was instrumental in the founding of the Board of Trade, the YMCA, Middle Georgia Fertilizer Co., Citizens Loan Co., and Dublin Lumber Co.

CPSIA information can be obtained
at www.ICGtesting.com
Printed in the USA
BVHW061538301121
622778BV00005B/506